Simply Dance

Tango and Paso Doble

Rita Storey

W
FRANKLIN WATTS
LONDON • SYDNEY

Before you start

Dancing is a great way to get fit and meet people. Wherever you live there are likely to be dance classes held somewhere nearby. There are some steps in this book that you can try to get you started. There are also some suggestions for clips of music to listen to on pages 28 and 29.

You do not need a special costume to learn to dance. A pair of comfortable shoes and clothes that let you move easily will be fine to start with. It is not a good idea to wear trainers when you are dancing as the soles grip the floor and make it difficult to turn your feet easily. Some dance studios have their own dress code, so you might want to check what it is before turning up to a class.

When you are dancing it is a good idea to wear two or three thin layers of clothing. At the start of a dance session you need to keep your muscles warm to avoid damaging them when you stretch. As you get warmer you can take off some layers.

Like any type of physical exercise, dance has an element of risk. It is advisable to consult a healthcare professional before beginning any programme of exercise, particularly if you are overweight or suffer from any medical conditions. Before you begin, prepare your body with a few gentle stretches and exercises to warm you up.

Dancing is getting more and more popular. Give it a try and find out why!

First published in 2010 by
Franklin Watts
338 Euston Road
London NW1 3BH

Franklin Watts Australia
Level 17/207 Kent Street
Sydney NSW 2000

© Franklin Watts 2010
Series editor: Sarah Peutrill
Art director: Jonathan Hair

Series designed and created for
Franklin Watts by Storeybooks
Designer: Rita Storey
Editor: Nicola Barber
Photography: Tudor Photography

A CIP catalogue record for this book is available from the British Library

Printed in China

Dewey classification: 793.3'3
ISBN 978 0 7496 9363 3

Picture credits
All photographs Tudor Photography, Banbury unless otherwise stated
Getty images p17; Clark Samuels/Rex Features p26;i-stock pp 5, 14, 16, 27, 28 and 29.
Cover images Tudor Photography

All photos posed by models. Thanks to Ryan Brown, Kimesha Campbell, Jake Thomas Chawner, Lauren Cooper, Emile Ruddock and Libby Williams

The Publisher would like to thank dance adviser Kate Fisher (www.katefisherdanceacademy.com) for her invaluable help and support.

Franklin Watts is a division of Hachette Children's Books, an Hachette UK company. www.hachette.co.uk

Contents

Ballroom dances

Tango and paso doble

Ballroom dances are performed by couples and recognised in competitions around the world. They are split into two groups: 'International Standard' and 'International Latin'. In International Standard ballroom dancing, a couple must spend most of the dance in a ballroom or **closed hold** (with both hands in contact). International Latin dances usually have a lot of hip action and rhythmic expression. They do not always have to be danced in a closed hold. The two partners in a couple may dance side-by-side, or even dance different moves from each other.

The tango and paso doble are both dramatic dances. The tango has its roots in **Latin America** but is now classed as an International Standard dance – the 'ballroom tango'. There is another version of the tango, called 'Argentine tango'. This has its own internationally recognised competitions. The paso doble is an International Latin dance.

The tango is a dance that originated in Buenos Aires, the capital of Argentina. It was danced in the back streets of the city by poor, working-class people, mainly Spanish and Italian immigrants. There were many more men than women in these areas – some figures suggest that men outnumbered women by nearly 50 to one. There was a lot of competition amongst the men in order to be noticed by a woman. One way of attracting attention was to be a good tango dancer!

In the early 1900s the tango began to be popular with the upper classes in Argentina. The dance was taken to Europe by Argentinian sailors and by wealthy businessmen who travelled abroad. It became so popular in the cafés of Paris that tango tea dances were held. The passionate nature of the tango shocked many people, and as a result the dance was banned in some places. Despite this the craze continued to spread. In 1913, the tango arrived in New York City.

Ballroom tango

In Europe the tango began to move away from its traditional roots in the 1920s. New steps were added, and the dance was defined and standardised so that people could compete against each other within a clear framework of rules. The sharp (**staccato**) head movements that we associate with the tango today, and the walking (**promenade**) steps that move the dance around the ballroom were both added at this time. This more standardised version of the tango is now known as the International, or ballroom, tango.

This couple is dancing a ballroom tango.

Argentine tango

The Argentine tango remained popular as a social dance in both Europe and Argentina. It retained the **improvisation** associated with the original tango, but over time other versions developed. With so many different versions, the argument about which style of tango is the correct one continues to be the subject of heated debate.

Tango styles

The Show tango A style of tango developed for film and stage performances. The moves are exaggerated and dramatic.

The tango Orillero An intimate form of the dance that moves very little from one spot and is danced in small spaces.

The Salon tango A style with travelling steps that make it more suitable for dancing in larger spaces, such as ballrooms.

Argentinians are very proud of the tango. Today in parts of Buenos Aires you can watch impromptu tango shows, as couples dance to entertain visitors to the city.

Ballroom tango – the basics

The ballroom tango is a walking dance. Rather than gliding across the floor, as in some other ballroom dances, in the tango the feet are 'placed'. Because of this, the tango is a good dance to learn when you first start ballroom dancing. The walks should be strong and proud and should reflect the music of the dance.

KEY

G	The girl's steps
B	The boy's steps

'count' Count the moves as you dance them. You can count out loud at first if it helps.

Tango walks

The **rhythm** of a ballroom tango is counted in slow and quick steps. There is no rise

Tango walks

slow   *slow*

1 Take a long step back on your right foot.

1 Take a long step forwards on your left foot.

2 Take a long step back on your left foot.

2 Take a long step forwards on your right foot.

and fall in the tango, instead the whole dance is done with bent knees. As the man walks forwards, his heel should touch the floor before the rest of the foot – just as in a normal walking step. This is called a **heel lead**.

Ballroom tango hold

In a ballroom tango the couple dance facing their partner, with both hands in contact (ballroom or **closed hold**). The woman's upper body leans back and slightly away from her partner. The position of the woman's hand is different from other ballroom dances as she tucks her thumb under the man's arm, with her fingers straight along his shoulder.

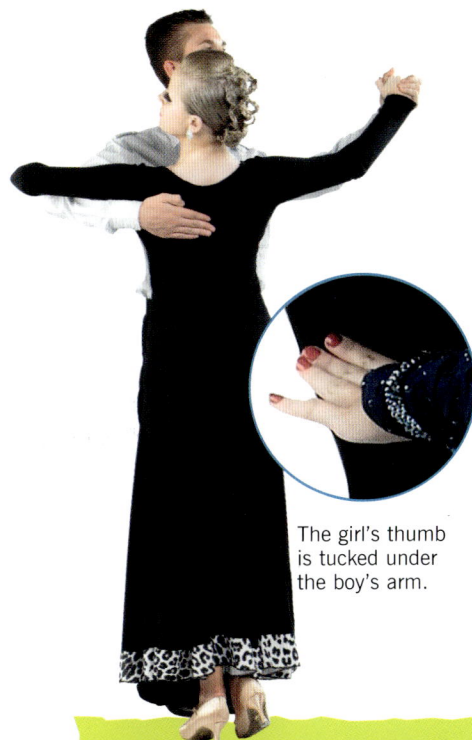

The girl's thumb is tucked under the boy's arm.

This couple are in a closed ballroom hold ready to dance the tango.

Progressive link

quick   quick

1 Step back on your right foot.

1 Step forwards on your left foot.

2 Step to the side with your left foot and turn your body to the right. This is called promenade position.

2 Step to the side with your right foot and turn your body to the left. This is called promenade position.

Ballroom tango steps

All ballroom dances have moves that are easily recognisable and which make them different from any other dance. In the ballroom tango the moves that display the character of the dance are the quick (staccato) head turns by the woman, and the dramatic tango walks and promenade steps.

Closed promenade

slow   *quick*

1 Step on to your right foot.

1 Step on to your left foot.

2 Step forwards and across with your left foot.

2 Step forwards and across with your right foot.

Promenade step

In the promenade step the couple remain in hold but instead of dancing forwards or backwards facing each other, they dance the same step walking side-by-side.

quick

slow

When you close your feet in a ballroom tango the ball of your right foot should be next to the instep of your left foot (girl), or the opposite way round (boy).

3 Step to the side on your right foot.

3 Step to the side on your left foot.

4 Close left foot to right foot.

4 Close right foot to left foot.

Contracheck

slow *slow*

2 Close left foot to right foot.

2 Close right foot to left foot.

1 Step strongly forwards on to your left foot.

1 Step strongly back on to your right foot.

Contracheck

A contracheck step is a stopping (or checking) movement. Although the beat is slow... slow, the movement should be strong and sharp as you step back and as you close.

Spanish drag

This step is a long step to the side and a controlled drag of the foot back into closed position. There is a quick head turn for both the man and the woman as they take the last step into promenade position.

Tango on stage and screen

There have been many important stage shows and films featuring the tango. In 1983 a show called *Tango Argentino* opened in Paris. This spectacular dance show was a huge hit. It revived interest in the tango after its popularity had been in decline since the 1950s. More recently, films such as *Moulin Rouge!* (2001), which features the song 'El Tango de Roxanne', and *Shall we Dance?* (2004) have all added to the popularity of the tango.

Ballroom dancing on television has never been more popular. *Strictly Come Dancing* in the UK and *Dancing with the Stars* in the USA have both been responsible for a new wave of interest in ballroom dancing as a hobby.

Spanish drag

slow

1 Step strongly on to your right foot.

1 Step strongly on to your left foot.

slow

2 Drag your left foot back in to your right foot.

2 Drag your right foot back in to your left foot.

quick

and Close left foot to right foot.

and Close right foot to left foot.

The 'and' **beat** is the moment when the feet close together after step 2. It should be a sharp, definite move.

slow

3 Step to the side with your left foot and turn your body to the right. With a strong staccato action turn your head to the right.

3 Step to the side with your right foot and turn your body to the left. With a strong staccato action turn your head to the left.

Putting it together

The dance steps on pages 6–11 can be joined together to make a routine if you follow the sequence shown below.

Tango walks (page 6)

Start with your feet together weight on the left foot (girl), right foot (boy).

slow   *slow*

1

2

Progressive link (page 7)

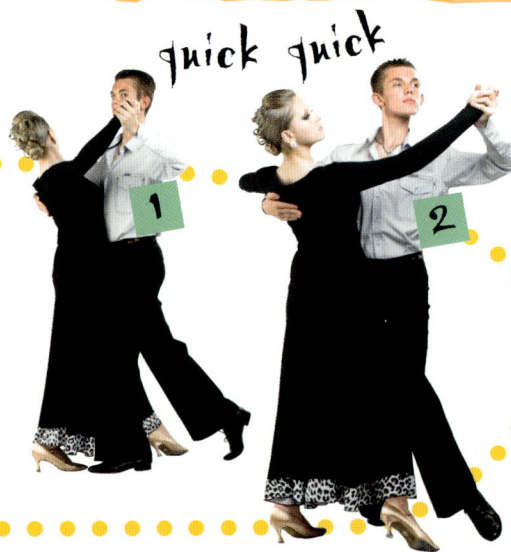

quick   *quick*

1

2

Closed promenade (pages 8–9)

slow   *quick*   *quick*   *slow*

1

2

3

4

Contracheck (page 10)

slow   slow

1

2

Spanish drag (page 11)

slow   slow   and   slow

1

2

and

3

Finish with another 'Closed promenade' (see pages 8–9) then start the routine again from the beginning.

Argentine tango

Unlike the more formal ballroom tango, with its set patterns of steps, the emphasis in the Argentine tango is on the emotional communication between the two partners.

The man must communicate what step to do next by a signal to his partner. She can choose not to follow his lead and suggest her own move. At times, the woman may be dancing completely different steps from her partner.

The Argentine tango hold
In the Argentine tango the upper body is quite still and the legs do most of the work. The hold is close in the upper parts of the body – almost cheek to cheek. The clasped hands push lightly against each other to maintain balance.

The walk
The Argentine tango is based on a walk, called *la caminata*. If you thought that walking was easy – think again! *La caminata* is not just any walk, it should be catlike – careful and deliberate, but also graceful and stylish. The walk must also interpret the music both in style and pace. Just as in ballroom tango, there is no rise and fall – the walk is on the balls of the feet rather than flat on the floor.

The basic steps
The basic steps in the Argentine tango are walking steps, turning steps, pauses and adornments (*adornos*).

In the Argentine tango the man takes the lead. His partner waits for a signal so that she knows what move to do next.

The Argentine tango is often danced in crowded places. Some steps, such as this back *corte*, are done on the spot until there is room to move on.

Competition tango

As dancers improve they often like to enter competitions to see how well they can perform against each other. Couples take part in ballroom dance competitions locally, nationally and internationally. If they win they may take home a cup or a prize, but for those who do not there is the enjoyment of mixing with other dancers and making new friends, as well as the excitement of performing in front of an audience.

Judging the ballroom tango

In the ballroom tango the routine should include promenades (walks) and link steps. The routine should be full of drama and passion and tell a love story through the dance. The footwork should be separate steps using heel leads for the forwards steps. The **head snaps** that are a signature move of this dance should be sharp and quick.

To dance a ballroom tango in a competition the boy wears a tail suit and the girl wears a long ballroom dance dress.

Performing the Argentine tango

The Argentine tango is more improvised than the ballroom tango. It has traditionally been danced socially rather than in competitions. People watch other dancers perform in cafés and bars, but the atmosphere is appreciative rather than competitive.

Some people want to be able to compete against other couples, so competitions for Argentine tango are now held. However, some people still think that the Argentine tango should not be danced in competitions as they make the dance too formal.

The Argentine tango is always danced with plenty of 'attitude'! In competitions, the dance is judged on the connection between the dancers and the way in which they interpret the steps.

To dance an Argentine tango, the girl's dress usually has a split or is short on one side to show off the complicated leg moves. The man's outfit is Latin American in style.

What is the paso doble?

The paso doble is a dramatic ballroom dance performed to music that has a march-like beat. Paso doble means 'two-step' in Spanish. While the characteristics of the dance are Spanish, the ballroom version of the paso doble was developed in France.

The paso doble is based on the steps of Spanish gypsy dances and it recreates the drama and movement of a Spanish bullfight. In each dance routine the man takes the role of the bullfighter (**matador**). Depending on the interpretation of the dance, the woman is either his cape, the bull or a Spanish dancer.

At a real bullfight the matador goads a bull into attacking him by waving a red cape. As the bull charges, the matador sidesteps and whisks the cape out of the way. In the dance, the man's moves are based on the matador's actions as he attracts the attention of the bull, then sidesteps the charge.

The paso doble became popular in Europe and America in the 1930s.

A matador walks into the bullring, ready to fight a bull.

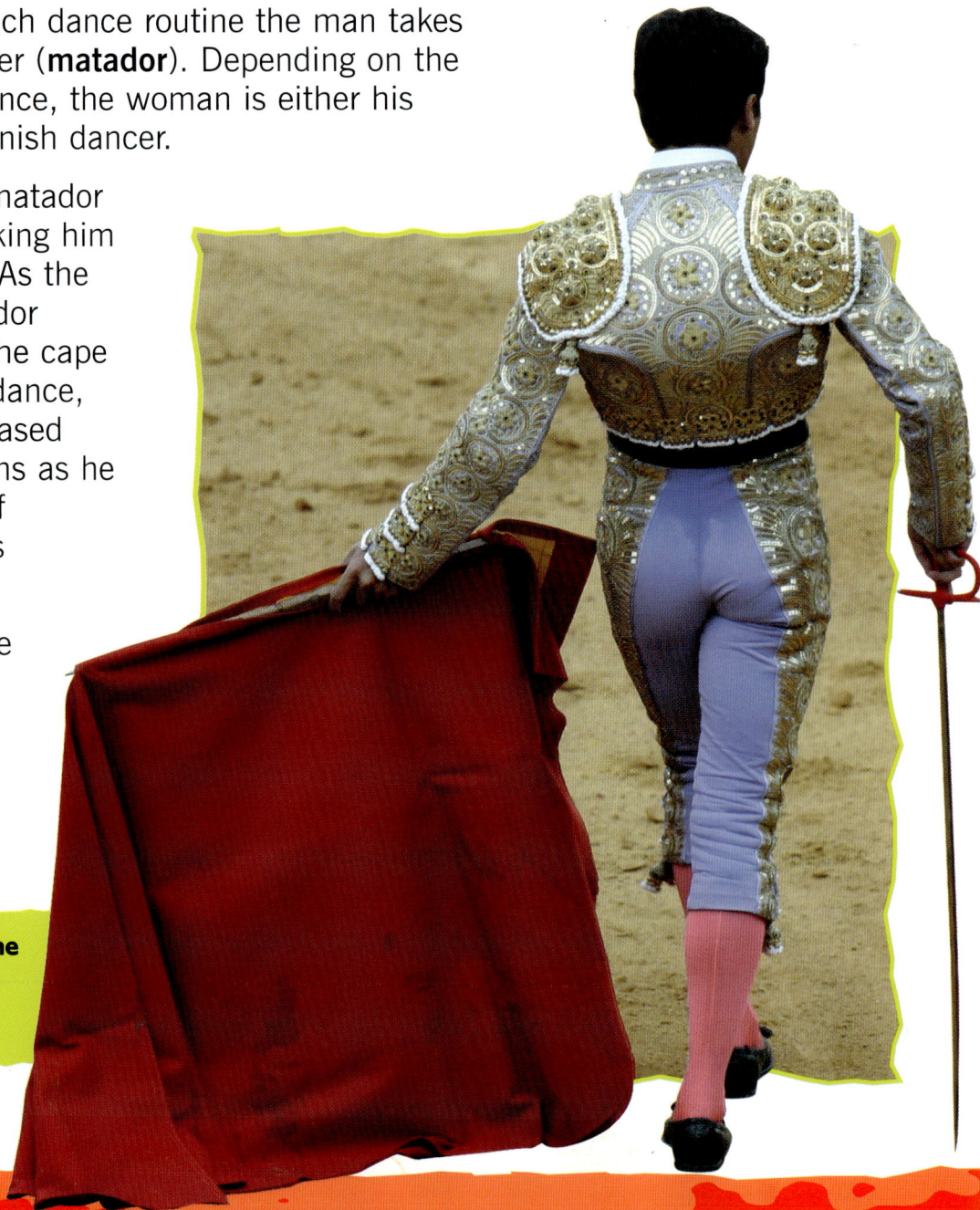

The French took the dance to their hearts and made changes to turn it into a ballroom dance. This is why most of the paso doble steps have French names.

The matador

When a man dances a paso doble he must take on the characteristics of a matador. He must exude confidence and power, but be agile and elegant. He must portray a sense of danger and bravery. He needs to have perfect timing and footwork, yet his moves should seem effortless and unhurried.

The moves of the woman in a paso doble are woven around the man. Her role is to complement the shapes he makes as he dances. Yet it is not a submissive role – she should look proud and strong.

Darren Gough and his dance partner Lilia Kopylova practise a paso doble for the TV show *Strictly Come Dancing*.

Unlike the other Latin dances, there is no hip movement in the paso doble. The dance contains *appels* (foot stamps). These are the stamps that a matador makes to get the attention of the bull in a bullfight. The paso doble is danced to a regular marching beat. The forward steps are done with a heel lead (see page 7). Unusually for a Latin dance, the paso doble is danced with a serious look rather than a smile.

The paso doble hold

Correct **posture** is very important in the paso doble. The man must have the posture of the matador – head upright, chest out and back arched. The hold is closed with the arms held high. The man's right arm is on the woman's left shoulder blade. The woman's left arm is on top of the man's upper arm.

This couple are in a closed Latin hold, ready to dance the paso doble.

Sur place

1–8

Step right, left, right, left on the balls of the feet and repeat.

KEY

G The girl's steps

B The boy's steps

Boy and girl steps

1–8

Step left, right, left, right on the balls of the feet and repeat.

Appel

For the **appel**, or foot stamp, stand high on the balls of the feet, then stamp or lower the foot.

Sur place

Sur place means 'in place' or 'on the spot'. It is a simple step from one foot to the other. The beat is a regular marching beat. When done moving either backwards or forwards the *sur place* step is called the basic step.

Chasse

Chasse steps are used in many different dances. *Chasse* means 'to chase'. In a *chasse* step one foot chases the other – step, close, step, close.

The dancers facial expressions should be serious when they are dancing the paso doble.

Chasse

one

two

three

four

1 Step to the side with your left foot.

1 Step to the side with your right foot.

2 Close right foot to left foot.

2 Close left foot to right foot.

3,4 Repeat steps 1 and 2.

Paso doble steps

The separation

Done to a count of eight this move represents the matador throwing his cape forwards and drawing it slowly back towards him.

The separation

one

1 *Appel* on left foot.

1 *Appel* on right foot.

two

2 Walk back strongly with your right foot.

2 Walk forwards strongly with your left foot.

three

3 Walk back strongly with your left foot. Release the left-hand hold.

3 Close right foot to left foot. Release the right-hand hold.

four

4 Close right foot to left foot.

4-8 Mark time (*sur place*).

five

six

Remember – the girl is playing the part of the cape. Her arm and leg movements can be strong and dramatic as the boy draws her back to him.

5

6

6

5-7 Take small strong steps back to your partner left, right, left.

seven

7

7

eight

7

8

8 Close right foot to left foot and bring your arm up back into hold.

21

The attack

one

two

1 *Appel* on left foot ('stamp').

1 *Appel* on right foot ('stamp').

2 Walk back strongly on your right foot.

2 Walk forwards strongly on your left foot.

The attack

The attack step is danced after the separation. It represents the moment when the bull has been provoked into attacking the matador. The matador holds his ground until the last moment and then sidesteps.

three

four

3 Sidestep to the left.

3 Sidestep to the right.

4 Close right foot to left foot.

4 Close left foot to right foot.

one

The drag

The drag

In the drag step the leg movements represent the actions of the matador as he holds his cape out and then draws it back to attract the attention of the bull.

two

2 Slowly draw your right foot towards your left foot.

2 Slowly draw your left foot towards your right foot.

three

3 Continue to draw your right foot towards your left foot.

3 Continue to draw your left foot towards your right foot.

four

1 Step to the side on your left foot. Bend your left knee.

1 Step to the side on your right foot. Bend your right knee

Paso doble at the movies

The film *Strictly Ballroom* (1992) is an Australian romantic comedy in which the featured dancers astound the audience with their version of the paso doble.

4 Close left foot to right foot.

4 Close right foot to left foot.

Putting it together

The dance steps on pages 19–23 can be joined together to make a routine if you follow the sequence shown below.

The separation (pages 20–21)

one

1

two

2

three

3

four

4

five

5

six

6

seven

7

eight

8

Once you know the steps, put on some music (see page 29), hold your head up high, and begin to dance the paso doble.

The attack (page 22)

one   two   three   four

The drag (page 23)

one   two   three   four

Chasse (page 19)

one   two   three   four

Start the routine again from the beginning.

Competition paso doble

The steps and routines of ballroom dances are set down in a syllabus that is taught in dance schools. Dancers can take graded exams, called medal tests. The syllabus contains all the steps you need to learn for each medal. Once you get your gold medal you are ready to take part in open competitions.

The paso doble in competition

The pasa doble is all about the shapes created by the moves. The judges are looking for the story of the bullfight, told in the dance, and for the connection between the dancing couple. The judges also look for excellent posture from the men, and either swirling cape moves or strong **flamenco** steps from the woman. There are marks for the **choreography** of the routine and the speed and timing of the steps.

Drew Lachey and Cheryl Burke dance a paso doble on the *Dancing with the Stars* tour.

Flamenco dancers perform to the accompaniment of hand claps and a Spanish guitar.

Paso doble costumes

Traditional costumes for couples dancing the paso doble are based on the colours and styles of flamenco and the bullfight. Red, gold, black and yellow are all popular, as are Spanish lace and embroidered materials. The costume for the man is often based on that of the matador: tight-fitting trousers and shirt in either all black, or black and red, together with a short jacket (bolero) with embroidered shoulders.

The costume for the woman can be short or long. Some dancers like to use the material of a full skirt to represent the swirling cape as they dance.

Flamenco

Flamenco is a style of Spanish gypsy performance that includes *cante* (song), *baile* (dance) and *guitarra* (guitar playing). The dancers use foot stamps and hand claps to express their emotions. Flamenco became popular and began to reach a wide audience during the 1860s when it was often performed at *café cantantes* (music cafés).

There are elements of Spanish flamenco in some of the moves in the paso doble. The woman's hand movements may simulate the action of playing the castanets – pairs of small wooden percussion instruments that are clicked together in the hands (see page 29). The *appel* or stamping move may also have its origins in flamenco.

Dance to the music

The music you dance to is very important. The regular beat, or pulse, of the music gives you the timing to move to. The rhythm and feel of the piece help you to perform the dance correctly.

Tango music

The tango was originally accompanied by a small group of musicians playing the guitar, flute and violin. Later the **bandoneón** began to be used and eventually became the favourite instrument in a tango orchestra.

The bandoneón is a type of square-shaped accordion with buttons called keys at each end. The concertina bellows in the middle are pushed and pulled to create the flow of air that makes the sound. The notes are changed by pressing the keys. The Argentinian bandoneón has 71 keys. Each key plays a different note depending on whether the bellows are opened or closed.

Dance music Ballroom tango

A list of ballroom tango music can be found on:
www.dancesportmusic.com/tango.html

Short clips for you to listen to:
www.ballroomdancers.com/Music/search_style.asp?Dance=Tango

Argentine tango

'Oblivion', Ástor Piazzolla
'In a Little While', U2
'Tango to Evora', Loreena McKennitt
'Libertango', Bond
'El Tango de Roxanne' ('Tango for Roxanne'), *Moulin Rouge* soundtrack
'Womanizer', Britney Spears
'Infiltrado', Bajofondo

A bandoneón being played.

Music for paso doble

The paso doble is traditionally danced to dramatic Spanish music. All sorts of instruments are used for paso doble music including **castanets**, **maracas** and the **claves**. These instruments give the music a traditional Spanish sound. One piece that has become linked with the paso doble is the gypsy dance (*España Cañi*). There are many versions of this piece of music, played with a variety of different instruments.

Dance music Paso doble

A list of paso doble music, including the gypsy dance (*España Cañi*), can be found on:
www.dancesportmusic.com/paso.html

Short clips for you to listen to:
www.ballroomdancers.com/Music/
search_style.asp?Dance=Paso+Doble

Other suggestions are:-
'Thriller', Michael Jackson
'Eye of the Tiger', Survivor
'Habanera', Charlotte Church
'Gotta Get Thru This', Daniel Bedingfield

The Spanish guitar (below), claves (bottom left) and castanets (bottom right) are all used to play traditional paso doble music.

Glossary

adornos In the Argentine tango, *adornos* are extra steps that 'adorn' the dance and make it more beautiful.

appel A tap or stamp of the foot.

bandoneón A type of accordion used to play tango music.

beat The regular pulse of a piece of music – like a heartbeat or a ticking clock.

caminata The catlike walk that forms the basic step of an Argentine tango.

castanets Pairs of small wooden percussion instruments that are clicked together in the hands.

chasse A dance step in which one foot chases the other – step, close, step, close.

choreography The arrangement and sequence of steps that form a dance.

claves A pair of wooden sticks, held one in each hand, that are struck together to accompany music and dancing.

closed hold When a couple dances with the partners facing each other, with both hands in contact. The arm positions are different for each dance.

corte From the Sanish word 'to cut', in the tango a *corte* is a lunging move done on the spot.

flamenco A style of Spanish gypsy performance that includes singing, dancing and guitar playing.

head snap A quick, sharp turn of the head.

heel lead A step in which the heel touches the floor before the rest of the foot.

immigrant A person who moves from one country to live in another.

improvisation A performance that is made up step by step without being rehearsed.

International Latin dances These are the cha-cha, jive, paso doble, rumba and samba.

International Standard dances These are the quickstep, slow foxtrot, tango, Viennese waltz and waltz.

Latin America The Spanish- or Portuguese-speaking countries of South and Central America.

maracas A pair of oval rattles filled with seeds or beans which, when shaken, are used as rhythm instruments.

matador The principal bullfighter at a bullfight.

posture The way a person holds and positions their body.

promenade A walking step.

rhythm The pattern of sounds and silences within a piece of music.

routine A sequence of dance steps.

staccato A short, sharp move.

sur place French for 'on the spot'.

syllabus A summary of all the steps you need to learn for each dance medal or grade.

Further information

DanceSport

Ten ballroom dances are referred to as the DanceSport dances. These dances are governed by internationally recognised rules and are danced in amateur and professional competitions around the world. There are five International Standard and five International Latin dances.

In the USA the American Smooth and American Rhythm correspond to the International Standard and International Latin classifications.

DVDs

See a list of the top dance movies from 1977 to the present day: www.boxofficemojo.com/genres/chart/?id=dance.htm

To watch a paso doble try: *Strictly Ballroom* (1992) PG

For a magical Argentine tango see: *Take the Lead* (2006) PG-13

For a taste of ballroom see: *Shall we Dance?* (2004) PG-13

Bandoneón on the web

You can see a bandoneón being played by the tango composer Ástor Piazzolla. The piece of music in the clip is called 'Libertango': www.youtube.com/watch?v=RUAPf_ccobc

Note to parents and teachers

Every effort has been made by the Publishers to ensure that these websites are suitable for children, that they are of the highest educational value, and that they contain no inappropriate or offensive material. However, because of the nature of the Internet, it is impossible to guarantee that the contents of these sites will not be altered. We strongly advise that Internet access is supervised by a responsible adult.

Dance classes

Find a dance class wherever you are in the world:

www.dancesport.uk.com/studios_world/index.htm